Button, Button
Where's the button?

Book Festival 1995

Button, Button, Where's the Button?

101 Button Games

Hajo Bücken

Floris Books

Translated by Polly Lawson

All black & white photographs and colour photographs on
pp. 8, 16, 22, 23, 31, 35, 50, 58, 59, 63, 70, 71, 74, 75
by Dieter Rex. Colour photographs on pp. 12, 13, 34, 42,
51, 54, 55, 62 by Ernst Thomassen.

First published in German under the title *Knopfspiele*
in 1986 by Heinrich Hugendubel Verlag, München.
First published in English by Floris Books in 1995

British Library CIP Data available
ISBN 0-86315-214-7

Printed in Belgium

⌂ Games suitable for indoors

♀ Games suitable for outdoors

Contents

Board games for buttons

Jumping on the button-wagon

The journey from the vague notion in an author's head to the finished book is a very long one, involving huge amounts of work. I still wonder why Thomas Kniffler did not just think that I had a button loose when I suggested a book of button games to him. On the contrary he encouraged me.

So here it is. Readers and players will have to decide for themselves whether it is any good. I can only say that ever since I started working on this book I have been travelling around with buttons in my pocket! If I'm ever in a situation with a group of people, where it would be fun to play a simple board game with no complicated paraphenalia, on a train for example, out come the buttons.

The 'button' (Old French *bouton* derived from the Latin *bottare* to thrust) is not just *a small knob sewn to articles of clothing* as a dictionary maintains. It lends itself to all sorts of games. Buttons can roll, slide and ride; they can be carried, piled up, juggled, jammed together, blown or flipped. They come in different shapes and colours and can be made of all sorts of materials. They are warm or cold, rough or smooth to the touch, and have different numbers of holes. Their variations are endless.

The result is that we can do an amazing number of things with buttons. This book only touches on some of the possibilities. The only rule where buttons are concerned is that they should not be used solely for the purpose of buttoning up!

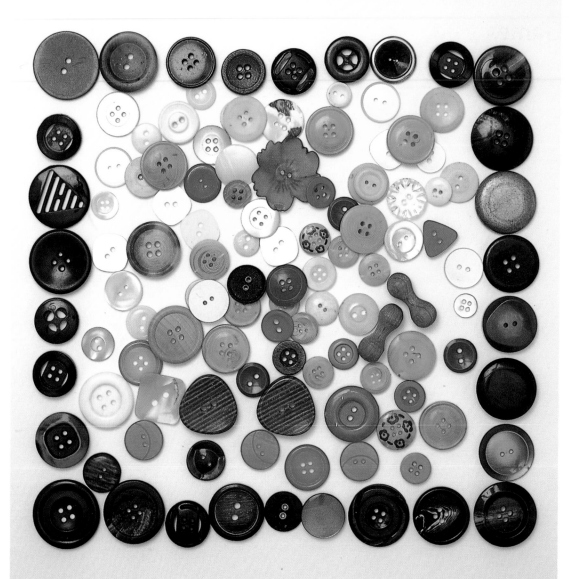

Games to get to know each other

Hunting the button ⌂♀

Hunting the button is the first sport for the future button-player. The hunt should be fun rather than too serious and intense, since there are all kinds of possible button sources. I began with the family sewing-box and immediately became infected by button-hunting fever. I was amazed by the different colours and shapes, the variety of materials, and the beauty or ugliness of the different buttons. You find yourself rummaging and rummaging, and not being able to stop, just like Donald Duck in his money pond.

Figure 2.

Finally you calm down a bit and find that you have a clearer idea of the buttons you want. Then you really start hunting in earnest. You have your eye on the ones you want, but since the best buttons are often achieved only through bargaining, you have to remain cool until you finally make off with your booty, knowing you have made a good haul.

You may still lack some flashy examples, such as a button in the shape of a heart or a cut glass cube? This is the moment to set off to small boutiques, or to the little antique shops round the corner. Pin down your friends with requests for buttons with three holes. Keep hunting till your hoard is as comprehensive as possible: complete with buttons with one to four holes, and buttons of all imaginable colours, materials and sizes.

Once you have amassed your button collection it's a good idea to keep them all in a special button basket.

Now you can start!

Ark button ⌂

This game, for any number of players, requires calm, sensibility and sensitivity.

All the players must imagine that they are going to leave a record of life on this earth for distant creatures from another planet. The only

materials they have for constucting this record are buttons.

Either taking their turns individually or as a group, the players select single buttons or pairs of buttons and form them into an ark or boat. When the ark is finished each player describes the selected buttons and says why they chose them and what they stand for.

Button trio ⌂

Each player shuts their eyes and gets three buttons stuck to their forehead with double-sided adhesive tape. They then have to find out the colours of these buttons. (One colour can appear more than once and there should be a total of only four colours in the game.)

Players then take turns to give each other clues, such as *I can see more reds and blues than greens and yellows on your head*; or *No colour appears more often than any other*; or *There is less of one colour than of the others*. In this way each player gives a clue without giving away anything directly. The players can take notes as they hear the clues.

When a player thinks they know what colour their buttons are, they declare them. If they are right they win the game. If they are wrong, they get a new set of buttons on their head and start again.

Figure 3.

Figure 4 >

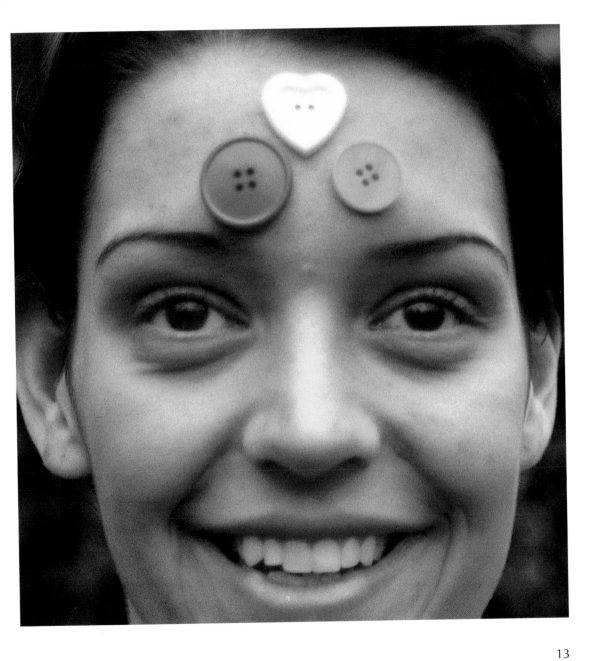

Button me ⌂

Each player chooses their favourite button from the button basket. It has to be a button which they think reflects their character and in which they can see themselves. Then each player lays down their button so that everyone can see it, and describes briefly how their button fits their character.

Button you ⌂

A variation of *Button me*. Each player selects a button without letting the others see it. A box or tin is turned upside-down and pushed along the floor or table to each player, so that everyone can slide their button under the box. The box is then removed and everyone has to guess who chose which button.

Betting your bottom button ⌂

Each player secretly selects five buttons from the button-basket. (The easiest way to do this is to pass the basket round to everyone.)

The first player places one button on the table, (assuming that other players have buttons of the same colour). Anyone who has a button of that colour has to 'declare' it and must pay the first player one button of the same colour. If no-one has a button of the same colour, and it must be *exactly* the same colour, the first player must put their button

back into the box. It is now the turn of the next player.

The game comes to an end when one player has no more buttons left and is therefore 'ruined.' Another round can then be played in which shape rather than colour is the deciding factor.

Button-holing ⌂

Lay all the buttons on the table. Each player silently chooses one of the other players to 'button-hole.' They then select suitable buttons and arrange them in such a way as to indicate or depict the player they have in mind. Everyone then tries to guess who each player is thinking of.

You can also write down the names of all the players on cards or pieces of paper. Shuffle the cards and lay them on the table face down. The first card is then turned over and each player makes a button picture of the person whose name has appeared (even the person him or herself!). This can lead to long discussions about the differences in the pictures, materials, colours and shapes.

Biggest, best and most beautiful ⌂

One player chooses a button without the others seeing it, checking that there is a similar button left among the remaining buttons. They then describe their button as if it were the biggest, best and most beautiful button in the world — a button that every one ought to have. As soon as someone thinks that they have guessed which button is being described they grab the similar one. If they pick the wrong one they lay it in front of them as a minus point. If it is the right one then the first player surrenders their button, putting it back in the basket. The player who has guessed successfully then secretly chooses a new button, and the game continues. Everyone should have a turn at choosing a button, even if they don't succeed in guessing. At the end of the game, the players with no penalty buttons in front of them are the winners and are appointed 'button-chiefs.'

I'll give you a button ⇧

Each player chooses a special button for each of the other players. The button should suit the person in question. The players then give the buttons to the people for whom they have been chosen.

As soon as each player has received all their buttons from the others, they place them on the table. Each player's collection of buttons is then looked at in turn and all the players discuss whether the buttons are suited to the person, and the possible reasons for the choice. Does the person in question agree with the picture the others have made of them, and do they find the shape, colour and material of the buttons indicative of their character?

Button search ⇧

This game requires there to be a relaxed and informal atmosphere between the players!

One or more buttons are hidden somewhere on the person of one of the players, while the searcher stands outside the room. The searcher is then called in and told how many buttons they have to find on whom. Then they has to search that person. Make sure you establish certain rules beforehand, such as *You are not allowed to undress the person.*

The life-story of a button ⇧♀

Each player takes a button and has to make up a story about the life of that button. The story can be exciting, gentle, unbelievable, crazy… whatever the storyteller decides.

For example, you might begin the story in this way: *Once upon a time there was a button. He was a very little button, and no-one took much notice of him. He only had two holes, and he was made of cheap plastic. In fact he was one of thousands turned out by a factory. But in spite of all this he was a very special button because anyone who had him on their clothes…'*

Button circle ⇧

The players sit on chairs in a circle. Take a thread long enough to go round the circle and thread some buttons onto it. Tie the ends together. Either the players must be blind-folded, or the button-circle must be under the table so that the players do not see the buttons.

Each player feels for a button and pushes it to their neighbour on the right, receiving at the same time a button from their neighbour on the left. Now the leading player describes one specific button which they know. The players have then to find out which button they have by feeling them.

and the others in order after it.

The other players then lay their buttons in the order which they think the first player has chosen. When everyone is ready they all take their hands away. The player whose buttons are in the order closest to that of the first player is the winner of that round.

The second player then orders their buttons and the game continues.

Button scenes ⇧

One player chooses some buttons and lays them out on the table so that they represent a situation. Other objects, such as matches and thread can also be used.

Once the situation has been built up the other players have to say what they think it is. For example, the buttons may represent heads, whole people, or objects. What is important are the proportions and the positioning of the buttons. For example, the buttons might illus-trate a family, a class at school, an office situa-tion, a chef at work, a football player, a boxer, a police-chase etc. etc.

Hit parade ⇧

The first player is given a random selection of five buttons. All the other players are then given a set of buttons matching those of the first player. The first player arranges their but-tons in order of preference behind their hand, with the favourite facing the middle of the table

Figure 5.   *Figure 6 >*

Button games for one

Button-gym ⌂

Keep fit — with buttons? No, that's asking a bit much! But button gym can provide a form of exercise for one person.

Using one hand, place five buttons on the finger-tips of the other hand. Then press the tips of the fingers of one hand onto the tips of the corresponding fingers of the other (thumb to thumb, forefinger to forefinger etc.), with the buttons in between, keeping the fingers firmly pressed so that the buttons do not escape.

Now sink down to the floor to sit crossed-legged like a tailor. Now bend to one side until you fall over, and then roll onto the other side. Now sit up again and take a breather. If you have had enough, try to stand up again without falling over. But if you want to do some more, try a forward roll! ...

Button building ⌂

Once you have collected enough buttons you can make a whole town with them. This is 'button-building'! You can use all sorts of different buttons to build the town: spires, high-rise flats and numerous other buildings begin to grow on the cardboard foundation on which the streets are drawn. Button-trees and button-ponds can be stuck on too, and even vehicles and people can be made out of buttons.

Utopian Buttonland ⌂

Once you have built a town you can go on to make a whole fantasy country. Indeed it is easier if you don't have to try to make things look too real! You can build fantastic buildings, and vehicles such as button-rockets, button air-planes, button-robots, all with a little 'button-imagination'!

Button mobiles ⌂

Button mobiles can become sparkling decorations! You have to hunt for the right buttons, whether silvery, coloured or transparent.

The 'beams' can be made of wooden rods or clothes-hangers. Threads hang down from these, holding the buttons, or other smaller hangers with further threads for buttons, or both. Move the threads along the beams to get the correct balance.

If you hang the mobile up by the window so that the sunlight falls on it then the whole room is filled with sparkling light.

Little boats ⌂♀

Figure 7.

As you can see in Figure 7 it's possible to find buttons in the shape of a boat. With these, in addition to ordinary buttons, you can make wonderful steamers. If you stick a drinking-straw through the button holes you can guide the boats without actually touching them.

Now all sorts of games can be developed: yacht races, piling up boats, or games of finger skill in which you have to move one or more boats from one table to another using only the straw.

The wooden boats can also be painted. You can shorten the straws to make masts on which sails can be hoisted. Then the boats really do sail on water and you can blow them along. You can also attach a thread to the stem of the boat as a tow-rope or painter. Load the boat up with as many buttons as possible. Then, taking the thread between your finger and thumb, you can tow the boat to a predetermined destination.

Button picture ⌂♀

Although the majority of buttons are round you can make mosaic pictures with them, as shown in the photographs. Figure 8 shows a small black sailing-boat. The boat is surrounded by

Figure 8 >

22

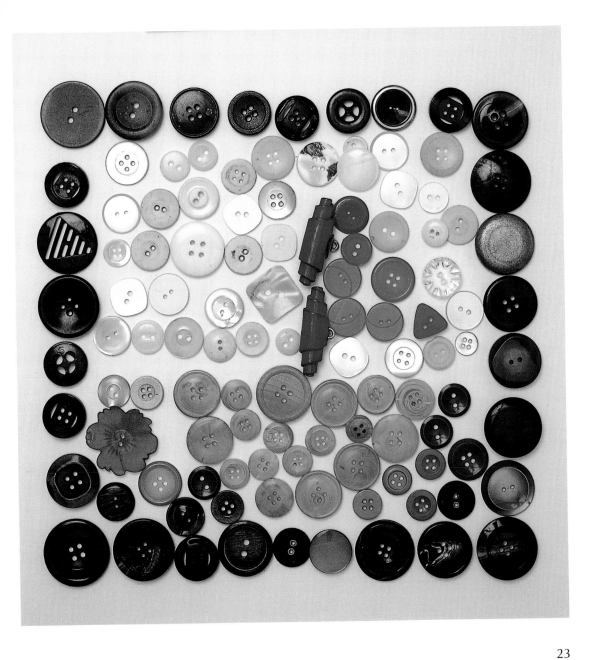

white buttons making a square, and the square is framed by large dark buttons. Better effects can be achieved with coloured buttons.

If you wish to make the picture a permanent fixture, you can either stick the buttons onto a piece of cardboard, or you can sew them onto paper, cloth or leather. This also gives you the opportunity to create further effects. Whole cushions can be decorated with button pictures. Also clothes, for example denim jackets or caps, can be attractively decorated.

Button art ⇧♀

Creating a button picture from an idea in one's mind obviously requires imagination, but the process comes to an end once the picture is finished, as for example when you depict a sailing boat on a blue background. However, you can require the observer to use their imagination creatively if your composition is not definitive and allows for an interpretation. Figure 1 (page 8) shows an image which allows one to make various mental pictures. Here it depends on the observer, on their mood and on whatever is preoccupying them at the time.

One interpretation of this picture is 'a pram,' another 'wheel-machinery,' and a third 'an ice-cream cone.'

Button animals ⇧♀

With buttons and pipe-cleaners you can create a whole zoo or farmyard of animals. Make the frame from the pipe-cleaners and thread buttons onto them to make round bodies. You could try a camel, glistening with all sorts of colours, a striped giraffe, or a multi-coloured snake!

Button music ⇧♀

Pass two threads though a button, one through each of the two holes. Trap one end of the two threads, between your feet and the floor for example, and hold the other two ends in your hand. Now with your free hand you can twist the button — the more the better. The threads then wind round each other. Take both the free ends in your hands, pull hard and the button will begin to spin, first slowly then faster and faster. Soon the swift rotation of the button will create music.

Finger puppets ⌂

Finger puppets can be made of wooden thimbles with buttons for the eyes, mouth and nose. Or you can use a white cloth or handkerchief for the doll's body. With the aid of thread and buttons a simple cloth can quickly become a flexible doll.

Games for two players

Hit the dot ⌂

Stick three little dots at each end of a rectangular table, about a hand's breadth from the edge. The dots can be in a line or in a triangle.

Each player receives three buttons plus a 'tiddly-wink' button. All the buttons should be the same size but they should be a different colour for each player. Choose buttons which are smooth and straight on top and a little rounded on the bottom. Lay the three buttons down, rounded side up, but hold the tiddly-wink button in your hand, rounded side down.

To start, place the three buttons on the three dots. The aim is to flip the three buttons onto the dots at the other end of the table as quickly as possible. To do this you press the tiddly-wink button against the edge of one of the other buttons to make it hop forward.

The following rules apply, though they can be altered if both players agree:
1 The first three turns must clear the dots.
2 You may not actively flip your opponent's buttons, but you may cause one of your buttons to push one of your opponent's buttons off course. Or you can flip one of your buttons so that it is in the way of one of your opponent's.
3 If you flip your own button off the table you must put it back on the starting point, but if you push your opponent's button off the table it must be placed on one of the dots.

Figure 9.

Blow the dot ⌂

Blow the dot is a strenuous variation of *Hit the dot*. In this game each player has a straw which they use to blow the buttons to their goals, that is if they don't run out of breath! The game can also be played with four players, either with all four players blowing at once, or, if you wish it to be less chaotic, with the players blowing alternately.

Figure 10.

Loading till you break ⌂♀

Ask someone to hold out their hand, preferably their steadier hand. Then begin to load buttons onto their fingers. Encourage them to turn their palm uppermost spreading their fingers out a bit, and hum, if they can, keeping their hand quite still.

Now start again, but tell the person with their hand out that this time they cannot use their thumb; the buttons will be loaded onto the four fingers only. They can help you decide which buttons will be the best ones to load on and in which order.

When you both feel you can't put on another button, you must take off all the buttons and put them on the table. Now another pair of players can have a go. See if they can get more buttons on than you did!

Or you can go on loading buttons till one falls off. Count up how many you manage to get on before any of them come off, and challenge the next pair to beat your total.

You could try putting buttons on each other's fingers at the same time. Each player must hold one hand quite still, for their partner to load buttons onto it, while at the same time, with the other hand, they pick up buttons from the table to load on to their partner's hand. See if you can manage this!

Figure 11 >

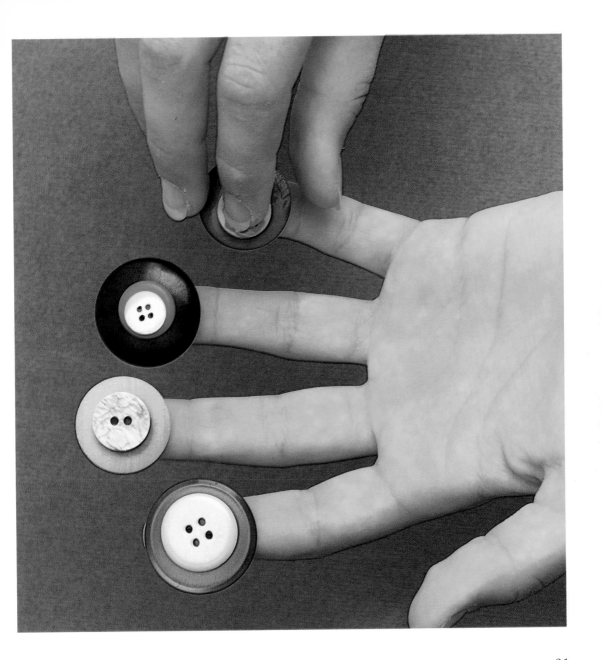

Handful ⌂

Two players each receive ten buttons (or fewer than ten, as long as they all receive the same number). Each player keeps the buttons in their hands, without laying any of them down. They must then divide the buttons between each hand without letting each other see what they are doing — quite a challenge! Then they lay one hand on the table with the other crossed on top of it.

Each player has to guess how many buttons their opponent has in their upper hand. They then open their hands. If a player has guessed correctly they gain a button from the other player. If they have guessed wrongly they have to give one to the other player. Once a player has only a few buttons left the game becomes easier for the other player, and the game ends when one player has lost all their buttons.

Dice button ⌂

The players make a long line of buttons. The first player places their counter on the first button at one end of the line, and the other player places their counter on the last button. Then they make up a rules about what happens at each button on the line: for example if you land on a white button you lose a turn, if you land on a red button you move one step forward.

The players take turns to throw the dice and advance along the line of buttons. The winner is the one who gets to the opposite end first. If a player lands on a button occupied by their opponent, they must go back the number of places they last scored on the dice.

You can invent all sorts of extra rules for this simple game.

Button head ⌂♀

Button head requires some patience as it involves decorating the head of a player with as many bright buttons as possible.

Thread the buttons onto the hair as if onto thread, twisting a few hairs into a thin thread (Figure 12). The buttons should be of various colours, shapes and sizes. Awkward buttons that keep slipping off can be fastened on with small, brightly coloured pegs.

There's no need to stop at the hair as you can go on to decorate the rest of the head with buttons. It's amazing how many buttons will fit in, on and around a head. You can put large buttons into the eye-sockets, to fit like a monocle, and smaller ones in and around the ears. You can even balance buttons on the lips.

Finally take a photograph as a record!

Push button ⌂

Each player has four buttons. Toss a coin (or a button) to see who begins. Each player lays a button down at their end of the table. The aim is to make your button hit your opponent's.

The first player pushes their button towards the other end of the table, with one shot. Now it is the second player's turn. The players continue to take turns until one succeeds in

Figure 12.

hitting the opponent's button. That player then collects both buttons and a new round is started. If a player pushes their button off the table the opponent wins both buttons. Play continues until one player wins all eight buttons.

An alternative rule: instead of taking turns, the player whose button is nearest to the edge plays.

Button switching ⭐

Put a button under each of three night light containers. The first player shows their opponent under which box they have placed each button. Then they cunningly switch the boxes around until the other player becomes quite

Figure 13.

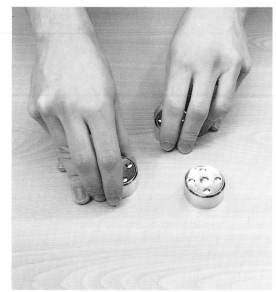

∧ Figure 14.

∨ Figure 15.

confused. The second player then has to say which container the button is under. If they are right it becomes their turn. If not, the first player goes on with their tricks.

Apex ⭑

This game players has a board consisting of 36 spaces arranged in an equilateral triangle, each side of which is made up of eight spaces (see Figure 16). Three sets of six buttons are used as counters, each set a different colour. The buttons are set out on the board as follows: the first button should be placed at one apex; the next two buttons, of the same colour as the first, go in the second row of the next apex,

and the last three buttons of that colour go in the third row of the third apex. The remaining two sets of six buttons are placed in the same way so that the final result is a triangle with a mini triangle of six buttons of the three colours at each corner (see Figure 16).

The aim of the game is to move all the six buttons of your colour into one corner-triangle, or alternatively into a triangle anywhere on the board. The moves are made as in Chinese Chequers: you can move a button to an adjacent empty place, or a button may jump over one other button to land on an empty space. Or you can make a series of such jumps.

With two players either may move the third colour to aid their own or thwart their opponent's moves. Alternatively, the game can be played with three players.

Figure 16.

Figure 17.

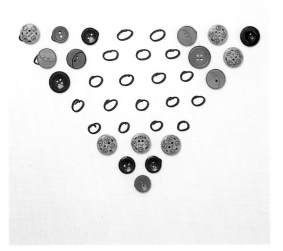

Pulling the thread ⇧♀

Take a button with two or four holes and pass two threads through it. One player holds one end of each thread between their thumb and forefinger, while the other player holds the other two ends, with the button lying in the middle. One player now carefully extends their arms. In this way the two threads are drawn away from each other and the button is pulled towards the other player. Once the button has arrived the other player spreads out their arms and the button goes back to the first player. The players can then make the button go back and forth, faster and faster.

Paralluya! ⇧♀

Again, the two players each hold the two ends of two parallel pieces of thread. Now take a larger button and lay it on top of the threads. Very slowly and carefully the players allow the button to slide along the threads from one player to the other. Both players have to watch the distance between the threads carefully. If they manage to slide the button the whole length of the threads they are a very good team. If they succeeed in getting the button to the other end of the thread and back again, they can breathe a sigh of relief and shout the magic word *Paralleluya!*

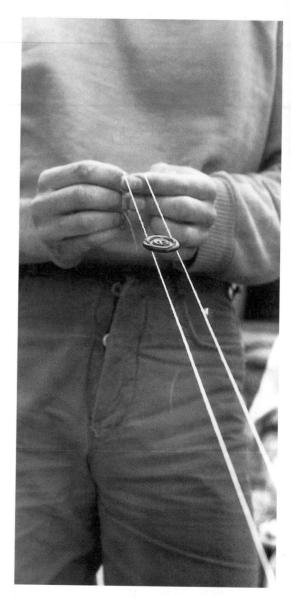

Figure 18.

Figure 19 >

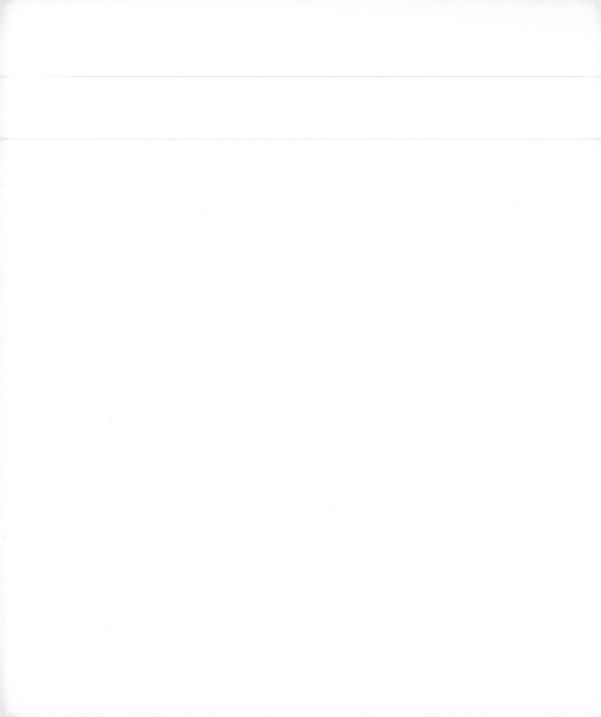

Games for many players

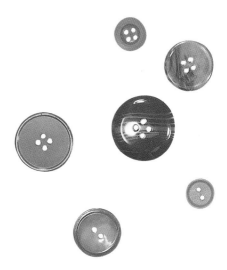

Button fingers ⇧♀

This game can be played individually or with other players.

Place a button (preferably one which is large and not too slippery) between your thumb and forefinger. Now, using only that hand, make the button go alternately under and over your fingers, right to your little finger, and back again, without resting your hand or arm on anything.

For a variation of this game which requires some skill: hold one hand up so that your fingers stand up vertically. With your other hand, place two buttons on the finger-tips of two out of the three middle fingers. The trick is

Figure 20.

∧ *Figure 21.*

∨ *Figure 22.*

now to bring the two buttons down towards the palm of your hand using only the hand which you are holding up, and only the three middle fingers of that hand. (It is best to practise with the buttons on the forefinger and middle finger first, and then on the middle and ring fingers.)

Button quads ⇧♀

A selection of buttons, including four of the same shape, are put on a plate. One of the players, blindfolded, tries to identify the group of four, by feeling.

To start with there should be four buttons which are easily distinguishable. Gradually the

Figure 23.

choice can be made more and more difficult. The button-quad can be chosen according to other criteria, for example there could be buttons made of leather, horn, wood, cloth, plastic, metal etc.

Who's got the button? ⇧♀

The players stand in a circle facing inward. All the players except one hold one hand open behind their backs. The remaining player (the 'button-layer') walks once round behind the others. This player places a button in some of the hands. In others they just pretend to place a button, or they place one and quickly take it away again. No-one is allowed to say anything or move their hand.

Each player must then take turns to say whether or not they have a button in their hand. They then show their hand. If everyone is right the button-layer must go round again, but if anyone has guessed wrongly they become the button-layer.

Button puzzle ⇧♀

This game can be played individually or with other players.

Try to obtain the following totals of button holes, using the smallest possible number of buttons, with one hole, two holes and four holes:
1 by adding or subtracting: 5, 15, 27, 100;
2 by adding, subtracting, multiplying or dividing: 15, 63, 19, 199;

3 by using each kind of calculation (adding, subtracting etc.) only once.

Now you can make up your own sums. You can also begin with a predetermined number of each kind of button.

Catch a button ⌂♀

Take a button from the table, throw it up into the air and catch it again. Throw it up a second time, pick up a second button from the table, and catch the first as it comes down. Now throw the two buttons up, pick up a third, and, quick as lightning, catch the other two. Then throw all three buttons up together and catch them.

Throw up two of the buttons, lay the third back on the table, and catch the other two as they come down.

Now throw one up, lay the other on the table and catch the first as it comes down, laying it finally on the table.

Button rows ⌂

Tip the button basket out onto the table. On the word *go* each player places twelve buttons next to each other as quickly as possible. Each button must have something in common with the button next to it. On the word *stop* everyone stops. Each player then has to explain their row. If a player has achieved twelve buttons in a row and has worked out special connections they are rewarded with applause.

Needle button ⌂♀

Place a button on a largish piece of cork. Poke needles through the button holes into the cork. The needles must stand straight up and should be parallel to each other.

Each player receives the same number of buttons. The challenge is to drop your button onto the button on the cork. Each player drops their button from the same height. Don't choose too great a height or the game won't work.

A tip: shut one eye and keep the other directly over the needles!

Demolition ⌂

Build a button tower as high as you can, towards the back of the table. As soon as you've built such a tower there is an awful temptation to knock it down or at least demolish it carefully, and this can lead to a game.

Each player takes it in turn to remove a button. For the first round they may use both hands. For the second only one hand. In the third round they have to blow off a button! In the fourth round they have to suck off a button with a straw.

Button on the back of your hand ⚲♀

In this game there are two of each kind of button. The players stand in a circle and each receives two different buttons, one for the back of each hand. Then one player can either reach over and take the button off the right hand of the player on their left, or, with their left hand, they can take the button off the left hand of the player on their right; thus always having to reach over their other hand. While doing this they must not let the button on their own hand fall off.

The players take turns to do this, and so the buttons are exchanged. Anyone who drops a button is out. The first player to get two of the same kind of button onto the back of their hand is the winner.

Prediction ♀

Dig six holes in the ground. Each player receives three buttons. They then take turns to try throwing a button into a hole, but first they must say which hole they are aiming for. (They may find they have been a bit ambitious.)

If a player gets their button into the hole which they are aiming for they get three points. If however their button lands in another hole by mistake they still get one point. A clear miss is a miss however and does not count.

Other variations are possible. For instance each player has six buttons and tries to get a button into each hole. Or the holes are numbered from one to six and the players throw a dice to see which hole they should aim for. If they succeed they get the appropriate number of points, representing a combination of the luck of the throw (of the dice) and the skill of the throw (of the button).

Wall breaker ⚲

Build a flat wall of four rows of buttons on the table or on cardboard. The largest buttons should be at the back, and the smallest at the front. Decide where the firing-point is to be. The first player lays a button on it, and uses their forefinger to flick the button towards the wall. (It is better to lay the shooting button face

Figure 24.

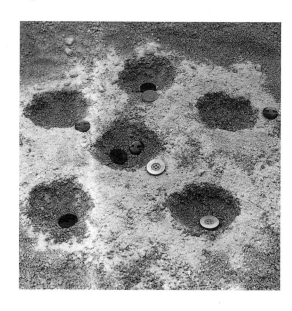

down, otherwise it will jump into the air or skid over the wall.) The players should count how many shots they need to break through the wall, so that their shooting button ends up behind the wall? The player who takes the least shots is the winner.

Players can take a pile of different buttons as ammunition to break through the wall. Then each player decides which button they will begin to shoot with. Once they have shot one button they cannot use it again, even if it lands in a position which strengthens the wall and makes the break-through more difficult.

Figure 25.

Figure 26.

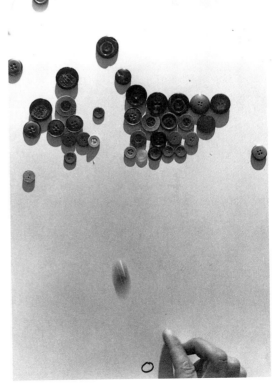

Tiddly-buttons ⌂

For this game select three or four larger buttons and lay them on the table. Place one upside-down (rounded side up), another can have a high rim, and the other(s) different potentially challenging features. These three or four buttons are the 'goal' buttons.

Each player receives one tiddly-button and three other buttons which should be the same type, but a different colour for each player. They should be placed on the starting point with their rounded sides facing down. Each player plays in turn, trying to flip their buttons onto one of the 'goal' buttons. Decide beforehand how many rounds will be played, or whether the winner is the one who gets all

Figure 27.

their buttons onto the 'goal' buttons. Now you can start, but remember that the buttons may skid or sail over their goals.

Button stick ⌂♀

Push a needle at an angle through one end of a bamboo stick. This will serve as a fishing rod. Now you need some different-sized buttons with one hole or better still with a loop, all in a bucket or bowl.

Each player is now given one minute to fish, and they fish out as many buttons as they can from the bucket. Or they can move buttons from one place to another with the fishing rod. Or the cane can be used as a guider with the needle forming an axle for button-wheels so that the buttons can be raced. There are hardly any buttons with holes right in the centre, so racing is quite tricky. Right from the start the button will tend to wobble or roll eccentrically and so badly that it soon come off the axle and you will have to hook it on again. The player who succeeds in bringing their button to the finishing line deserves a prize.

Button feeling ⌂♀

Select about eight buttons of different shape and material and put them on a plate or into a bowl. Study them carefully.

After this you must be blindfolded and must identify the buttons by feeling them. When you have become a master at this you must describe in detail whichever button you are

Threading buttons ⇧♀

Each player has a thread and the same number and type of buttons laid in front of them. On the word *go* everyone tries to thread their buttons as quickly as possible. As soon as they have threaded all their buttons, the player must take the two ends of their thread in their hands, shake the buttons into the middle of the thread and twirl them round once like a skipping-rope, finally letting the buttons run off again onto the table. The first player to do all this is the winner.

Figure 28.

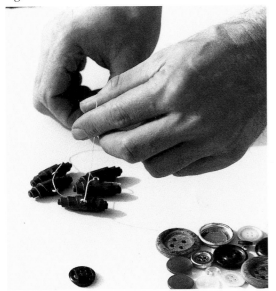

Keep a cool button! ⇧♀

A little game for two players, or more (in pairs).

Place a button between the tips of your noses and try to sit down, stand up, walk or crawl together.

Sit down on chairs facing each other. One person lays a button on the top of their foot and tries to pass the button onto their partner's foot. You are not allowed to use your hands. This is quite an acrobatic feat! Now pass the button back onto the first person's other foot, and back to the second person's other foot. Finally the button should go back to the first person's first foot. Done it? I don't believe it! There's a button lying on the seat of the chair! Lift the button with only one finger and bring it to another chair. Mind you don't drop it as you get it off.

Now the buttons should all be in a bucket. Fish them out with a spoon and take them to another bucket a short distance away. Record each player's time with a stop-watch. For every dropped button add three penalty seconds.

Press button ⇧♀

The players stand beside each other to form one or several chains. The player at the head of the chain has a button placed on the tip of their forefinger. The next player in the chain presses their forefinger onto the button. Then the two players turn their hands over so that the button now lies on the second player's forefinger. The first player takes their finger off carefully, while the third player stands ready. In this way the button travels the length of the chain. If the button is dropped the chain of players must start again. Once the button reaches the end of the chain the game is finished. Or it can be made to travel back to the beginning again.

Button-quartet ⌂

A game for three to ten players.

The players sit round a table. Pick out some really small buttons, one for each player, and lay them out in the middle of the table. Remove one, so that there is one less than the number of players.

Now take some ordinary buttons, enough for a set of four of the same for each player. Mix the buttons up thoroughly and deal them out. Each player puts their four buttons on the table, covering them with one hand. When everyone is ready the first player gives the command *pass*. Each player then passes one of their buttons, keeping it covered with their hand, to their neighbour on the left. On the command *take,* the players leave go of the button they are passing and pick up the one coming from their right.

The aim of the game is to get four buttons of the same kind — a 'quartet.' The buttons continue to circulate until one person gets a set of four. They then take their hand off their buttons and grab one of the mini-buttons in the middle of the table. Immediately everyone else tries to grab a mini-button. The player who is too slow and fails to do this is out. Then one of the sets of four buttons is removed from the game, the

Figure 29.

buttons are shuffled and dealt out again and the mini-buttons, minus one, are replaced in the middle of the table for the second round. After each round a player drops out, and one set of four buttons, plus one mini-button, is removed from the game. Eventually there will be only two players left. They play a round and the winner is the one who grabs the last mini-button.

A variation: each player is told which quartet they must collect. This makes the game more tactical since more than one player may be trying to collect the same quartet.

Shove-ha'penny ⌂

This is actually a variation of the old English coin game called *Shove-ha'penny*.

Each player receives the same number of similar buttons. Draw six parallel lines on a piece of cardboard or wood. Each field between the lines is given a value.

The players now take turns to fire their first button from the starting line with the aim of landing on the highest scoring field. However, they are not safe there: another button can push the first off the field. If a button lands on the line between two fields it scores according to the higher field. Beyond the 25 it scores nothing.

The game can also be played back to front. Each player takes it in turn to push a button from the opposite starting line. It is quite easy to land on the 25. But each successive button pushes the first mercilessly towards a lower scoring field.

Figure 30.

Figure 31.

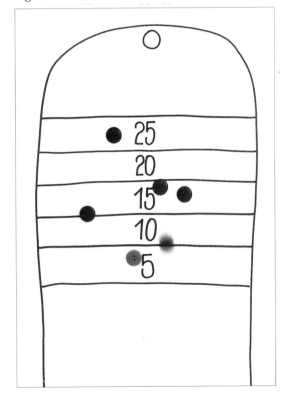

Button holes ⇧♀

Cut out some photographs from magazine advertisements and stick them onto some cardboard. Now cut some holes in the photographs in suitable places. Stand the placard up against a chair or armchair. The game consists of trying to throw your buttons through the holes. The holes should be different sizes, and appropriate scores can be awarded for them.

Button skin ⇧♀

You really need a carpeted floor for this game.

The players are blindfolded. With bare feet they walk over the floor and feel for the buttons which have been strewn there. They pick up the buttons with their toes, pass them into their hands and put them in their pockets.

A variation is for the players to be given

Figure 32.

buttons and, still blindfolded, they have to collect similar buttons, putting the wrong buttons back on the floor with their toes. Each player has to find four or five of their 'own' buttons.

Ninepin button ⌂

Draw nine button positions on a piece of card (see Figure 33). Place buttons on these positions. Each player has three buttons which they flick, one after the other, against the buttons, which serve as ninepins. You can use various kinds of buttons and decide on different values for the different ones.

The photograph shows the ninepin buttons face-up, but this can make the game rather easy, so you may wish to turn the buttons over so that the rounded side is uppermost. This means that they cannot be pushed off their points so easily.

Catch the button ⌂

Form two teams, each with at least two players. Each team decides who is the 'flicker' and who is the 'catcher.'

A starting line should be established on the table and one of the flickers places a button ready on this line. The catcher from the other team stands ready at the other end of the table. When the catcher shouts *fire!* the flicker flicks the button. They may send it anywhere on the catcher's side of the table. If the shot goes inside these limits the catcher must catch it to score a point. The catcher also scores a point if the button goes wide and falls off the side of the table. If the catcher fails to catch the button the flicker scores a point. The round lasts until everyone has had a turn of flicking and catching. Then the score is totted up.

You can make the game more difficult for a practised catcher by not allowing them to give the *fire* command, and allowing the flicker one minute during which they may fire at any time. Everyone must keep completely quiet because this variation requires the greatest concentration.

Figure 33.

Tortoise, flatfish, elephant ⌂

The members of one team sit beside each other at one side of the table, and the other team at the opposite side. A team must consist of at least two players, but not more than five. The starting team receives a button. The members of the team then decide who should have the button, and pass it below the table to that person, who then closes their hand over the button. The other team then gives a command for the way in which the button-players should bring their hands onto the table. The three commands are: *Tortoise, Flatfish* or *Elephant.*

On the command *Tortoise* the players put their closed fists on the table.

On the command *Flatfish* they lay their hands flat on the table, with their palms facing down.

∧ *Figure 34.*

On the command *Elephant* they must lay their hands on the table in the shape of an elephant. This is done in the following way: hold your hand with the fingers pointing down. The thumb and little finger form the hind legs, the forefinger and ring-finger the forelegs, while the middle finger points forward to make the trunk. The tips of the fingers (except the middle finger) land on the table.

You can also give the command *Double elephant!* Then each player must place one elephant hand on the back of the other.

The player with the button must try not to reveal which hand the button is under. Considerable skill is needed to achieve this!

The team which is guessing gets three tries, but they must all agree on each guess. If they guess right, they score a point, and it is their turn to hide the button (see Figures 34-37).

∨ *Figure 35.*

52

Red button — red face ⌂♀

Throw a green button into the air, and before you catch it again, pick up as many white buttons from the table as you can. The snag however is that the white buttons are mixed in with red ones. A white button scores one point, a red button minus five. So don't get the red button as you'll end up with a red face!

Roll button ⌂♀

Whatever can stand should be able to roll as well. So encourage everyone to choose three buttons from the button-box. The buttons

∧ *Figure 36.*   ∨ *Figure 37.*   *Figure 38.*

should be able to roll well. Now take a board 4" to 8" (10–20 cm) wide and lay it on a gentle slope. Try rolling your buttons down the slope. Can you get a button to roll the whole way down? Do you have a button that won't roll at all or always rolls off the edge? You can lay bets with your buttons.

— How many buttons are there?
— How many have one, two or four holes?
— How many are dark-coloured and how many light-coloured?
— What shapes are they?
— What kind of surfaces do they have?
— What colours are they?

Memory button ⌂

Another game requiring an immediate solution. It can be played with several players.

Have some buttons ready in a bowl and look at them carefully. Turn the bowl over or cover it, and then try to answer the following questions as accurately as you can:

Figure 39.

Target button ⌂

Draw or stick three targets near the end of a table. Each player has two buttons to use as counters and one flip-button. They start from the opposite end of the table and take turns to flip their counters. Obviously the aim is touch the aiming mark with a counter, but to win the

Figure 40.

game a player has to get *both* their buttons onto the mark. It is therefore necessary to use some tactics! You can cause your button to hit an opponent's and drive it away from the mark, but be careful: if you send an opponent's button off the table your own button goes back to the beginning, and you may lose the game.

Try and guess ⇧

Pour a number of buttons into a wine glass or jar. The players have to guess how many buttons there are, or they can guess the number of holes in the buttons, or how many there are of each colour. Then they can guess how much 10, 50 or 100 buttons would weigh.

Figure 41.

Button relay race ⇧♀

Two teams line up beside each other in files. A chair is placed at the end of the run for each team. A similar set of different buttons is placed on the chair for each team. On the word *go* the first player of each team races to the chair, picks up a button and runs back. The second player takes the button from the first player, holds onto it firmly, runs to the chair, adds a second button to the first, and runs back. The game goes on in this way until the last player of one of the teams comes back with all the buttons.

It is a good idea to time this, and if either team drops a button they incur a penalty of one minute.

Button rally ⇧♀

Each member of a team is given a different task. The team can vote for who does which task. The teams line up so that the players with the same task are in the same order. For example, a task might be to run the allotted distance with a button on the tip of your forefinger, or between the tips of your two forefingers; or with a button on each finger; or with a button on the tip of your nose; or with five buttons held between the fingertips of two hands pressed together.

Magic straws ♀

Each player is given a straw and appointed one chair with three buttons placed on the seat. There is also a 'goal-chair' and the aim for each player is to move their three buttons, one by one, onto the goal chair. They are only allowed to use the straws to do this and are not allowed to touch the buttons. They have to put one end of the straw in their mouth, press the other end against the button, and suck. They must then run quickly to the goal-chair and deposit their button. This is not easy as the buttons are quite heavy to hold just by sucking. If anyone drops their button on the way they must suck it up again.

Figure 42.

Nailing the button ♀

Lay a plank on two wooden blocks, or a board on the table. Each player is allotted a portion, about shoulder-width, of the plank. Then all the players take a hammer, seven nails and three buttons, one with one hole, one with two holes and one with four. On the word *go* the players hammer their nails through each button hole so that all the buttons are nailed to the plank. The winner is the first to get all their nails in.

If the plank is too short or the simultaneous hammering turns out to be too hair-raising, the players can of course take it in turns and be timed.

Figure 43.

Button wall ♀

This game is by no means a new one. It used to be played with pennies on runied walls. Each player receives three similar buttons. The first player stands behind a line and tries to throw their buttons as close to the wall as possible. Then the next player has a go. If they do not beat the first player's throws they can try a second and maybe a third time.

You can arrange the scoring so that only the best throw counts, or you can work out the distances of all three buttons, and then the shortest total distance from the wall wins. The player with the worst overall result must surrender a button. If a player loses all their buttons they are 'out.' Or they continue with three buttons and other buttons can be given to the winner of each round as prizes The winner is then the one who is the first to achieve an agreed number of prize buttons.

Button mosaic ♀

Hit several similar buttons carefully with a hammer so that they are broken into bits. The game is to fit the pieces back together again, as in a jigsaw puzzle. You'll find it's a bit more difficult than you might think. (The buttons can all be the same colour or they can be mixed. But if they are mixed it is still important to have several buttons of each colour otherwise it's all a bit too easy!)

Clothes buttons ⌂♀

This game must be a surprise so that no-one is prepared. Each player receives a towel which they drape across themselves from their neck to their legs. Now each player has to say how many buttons each of the other players are wearing on their clothing, and how many buttons there are altogether. Make sure no-one rips off any buttons to make their guess correct!

Figure 44.

Button-combi ⌂

Draw a square containing sixteen little fields on a piece of paper. Number the fields from 1 to 16 (see Figure 45). One of the players acts as umpire and does not play in this round. The umpire places sixteen buttons on the fields, while the other players keep their eyes closed. The umpire then says *Off we go* and the players open their eyes and have to do calculations based on the number fields on which certain buttons are placed, according to the umpire's directions. For example: *The lowest two-holed triplet, and the highest one-holed pair.*

The *lowest triplet* here means that the players must find out the numbers of all the fields on which the two-holed buttons are placed and

add up the three lowest of these numbers. They add this total to the total of the two highest scoring fields which hold buttons with only one hole (the *highest one-holed pair*).

All sorts of similar calculations are possible. The umpire is also allowed to bluff, giving a sum which is quite impossible, but which the players still have to try.

Harlequin ⌂

You will need twelve buttons: four sets of three similar ones. Place them on the board as in Figure 46. You are not allowed to occupy or jump over the middle square. Otherwise each player can move any button. The winner is the

Figure 45.

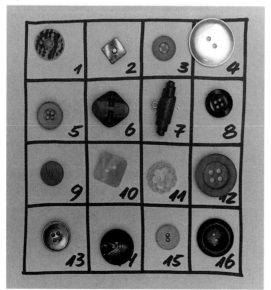

Figure 46.

one who can get three similar buttons onto any three adjoining squares, not necessarily in a straight line. The moves are made as in *Chinese Chequers,* either to a an adjoining square, or over another button to an empty square.

Hide the button ⌂

Each player has a collection of the same number of buttons. Each collection should be easily identified with its owner. The players then take it in turn to hide their collection around the room while the others wait outside.

Once everyone's buttons have been hidden the players sit round the table. Each has a pencil and paper. Each player takes it in turn to give the others a clue about where one of their buttons is hidden, and the other players make a note. No-one is allowed to ask questions. Each player may give as much or as little of a clue as they want. When all the clues for all the hidden buttons have been given, each player writes their name at the top of a fresh sheet of paper and underneath they write down where they think all the other players' buttons are. The pieces of paper are then collected together and marked.

The aim is to reveal just enough with your clues to enable some players to guess the hiding place, without getting up to search for them.

Each player scores one point for each successful answer. If no-one, or only one player, finds where a button is hidden the hider of that

Figure 47.

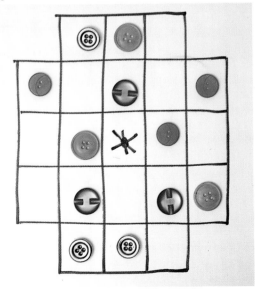

Figure 48.

button loses a point. The hider also loses a point if everyone guesses a hiding-place. In all other cases a player gets an extra point for each of their hidden buttons.

Button golf ♀

The first thing you have to do is prepare the button golf course (Figure 49). It should be as wild as possible. Dig bunkers on slopes, behind pools, or under stones. Put the holes on top of walls or under fences, marking them with flag poles, flags or chalk. It is up to the players to make the course interesting. For instance you can have bridges under which you have to send your button; high obstacles over which players have to climb and send their button; button-slides and so on.

Each player has one button (If you like you can have more than one so that you can use some for practising on the way. Experts should have only one, however.) Send your button off from the first tee towards the first hole and always count the number of strokes for each hole.

After the first trial round you can establish par for each hole and award handicaps for each player. Records can be made and championships arranged. I wonder who will be the first button golf world champion!

Figure 49.

Button pot ♀

Place a pot or container some distance away as an aiming point for throwing buttons. It will be easier for the players to get the buttons in if the pot slopes outwards, and a pot on the ground is easier to fill than one set up on a wall.

You can of course set up a whole series of pots with the smallest to the front and the largest to the back. Or you can set them up like ninepins and give them different values.

Or you can throw the buttons and challenge another player to catch them with their pot. You can hit the buttons back and forth with pans for rackets, as in badminton. Or throw one button into the air, followed by more and more and catch them in your pot.

Or two players stand opposite each other. Each holds a pot in which there is a button. On the word *go* both players sling the buttons out of their pots and catch the opposite buttons, also with their pots.

Button watchman ⌂♀

The button watchman sits down cross-legged behind the plate with the buttons on it. He is then blindfolded. Button-thieves now creep up softly and cautiously and try to steal the buttons from the watchman. The watchman defends the buttons by moving his arms to catch the thieves. See if they can still get through. If a button has been stolen the watchman takes even greater care to prevent the others from getting at the buttons. See how many buttons the thieves can steal in a set time, say five minutes? Someone else can then have a turn at being the watchman, and the first watchman can become a thief ...

Blindman's button ♀

∧ Figure 50. ∨ Figure 51.

This is an amusing variation of the game just described. One player is given a pot to hold in their hands. Then they are blindfolded. The other player stands about three yards away and has a number of buttons. This player calls to the blind man saying that they are going to send him a button. They throw one to him, in a high arc. The blind man judges where the thrower is by the direction of their voice.

The aim is to catch the button in the pot, but if a button finally does lands in the pot it can easily shoot out again, so the catcher must concentrate really hard. If they hear even the slightest noise coming from their pot they must make a shaking movement, so that the button hitting the inside of the pot does not spring out again immediately.

Button-factory ⇧♀

Using adhesive tape, stick a button on to the middle finger of one hand so that the button projects a good bit beyond the finger-tip. It should then be easy either to make the button fall back with an imperceptible flip of the fore-finger or to flick it up again with the thumb.

We now have a button-factory. Flip the button up and pretend to take it away with your free hand (making it fall back), and pretend to put it in your trouser-pocket. Then you can 'manufacture' as many buttons as you want in this way. You can conjure up buttons from the most unlikely places amongst the audience; out of ears, collars, clothes, etc. Just take care your button is properly stuck on!

Figure 52.

∧ *Figure 53.*

∨ *Figure 54.*

Sheepy button-head ⌂

Each player receives the same number of buttons of the same kind; for example, buttons with a specific number of holes, buttons made of different colours. It's best to play this game with two lots of twelve counters, made up as follows: three yellows, three reds, three greens and three blues, with a one-holed, two-holed and four-holed button of each colour.

Put the twenty-four buttons in a bag. Each player draws out their buttons without looking. If there are two players they each draw twelve, three players each draw eight, four players each draw six. Each player places their buttons behind their left hand and takes it in turn to put a button in the middle of the table. Players must follow suit (that is, they must lay down a button of the same colour as the previous one). If they cannot follow suit, they may use a different colour. A trump colour can be agreed, which beats all the other colours, but only when a player cannot follow suit.

To score, buttons with more holes score over those with less. A lighter coloured button scores over a darker one. The second identical button (same colour, same number of holes) scores over the first. When the last button has been played, everyone counts up the points they have scored, each button hole counting as one point.

This game can be extended in all sorts of ways. For instance a solo challenge in which one player, who thinks they can win the most points alone, plays against all the others. Or the two players who both have, for example, the yellow buttons with four holes, go into partnership.

Figure 55.

Button tower ⌂

You need a steady hand for this game. See who can build the highest tower.

First decide whether the buttons are to be specially selected for their building potential or taken out of the button basket at random. Each player must be given the same chance.

Everyone must keep perfectly still, so that the first player can concentrate. They select their buttons and build their tower. It must be as stable as possible because it is going to be very high. Each builder gets three goes, but they can stop after the first go if they think their magnificent edifice is high enough!

Now another player can count the number of buttons in the tower, or measure the height

with a ruler, depending on which method has been agreed beforehand.

There are plenty of variations on the button tower theme. A tower can be built by a team of two or three people, each taking it in turn to place a button. Or the tower can be taken down again by the same player or their partner. That may sound easy but it can be more difficult than the construction. Or the builder can be required to use their left and right hands alternately, or both hands simultaneously. Finally, the demolition can be blown down instead of being removed piece by piece.

Button poker ⌂

Up to five players sit around the table. Each player receives four buttons. They put between none and four of them in their right hand which they then lay closed on the table. In turn each player has to say how many buttons are in their own hand. Once a number has been said the next players may not say the same number.

Then each player has to say how many buttons there are in total in the hands around the table.

The aim is to get rid of one's own buttons first. The player who has guessed the right total can put away one of their buttons. If, however, they have guessed the correct total excluding their own buttons, they can discard two buttons. Now it seems obvious that if you subtract your own hand from the total you have the total excluding yours. But don't trust that poker face ... you can deliberately give a false total so that the others will not find out how many you have got.

If there are four or more players we recommend that the two button figures which each player gives are noted, otherwise you will land up in a muddle.

Button bowls ⌂

This game is played on a smooth table top. The first player sends their button sliding along the table, wherever they want it to go. This button becomes the 'jack button.' Everyone then receives three buttons. These should all be the same size but a different colour for each player. Now the players take it in turn to slide or 'bowl' their buttons so that they come as close to the jack-button as possible. They can also block their opponents' buttons or knock them out of the way.

The player who placed the jack starts the bowling. If a button falls off the table it is out of the game. If anyone knocks the jack off the table they must take the last place in the round and the jack has to be replaced by the first player in a convenient position.

There are endless variations on this game. Teams can play against each other. Or each player can take their three shots at one time. You can also lay an edging round the table so that you can bounce them off the edging.

From head to foot ⌂♀

Since a foot is capable of movement it can be used in all sorts of games which we might not immediately think of. Here are some examples:

Place a button on top of your foot and then kick it up into the air so that either you yourself or another player catches it. Or you can kick the button (or fling it with your foot) as far as you can, perhaps over an obstacle.

Place a button on top of one foot and hop a certain distance on the other foot without dropping the button.

Sit on a chair, put a button on each foot and flip them away. See if you can pick up the buttons with your bare toes and carry them somewhere else?

Some of the other games of skill described in this book can be played with the feet too.

One away, one in ⇧

Lay out a dozen buttons in front of a player. Give them some time to look at the buttons, and then ask them to close their eyes. Take one of the buttons away and replace it with another. The player opens their eyes. See if they can tell which button has been exchanged.

Alternatively you can lay out sixteen buttons in four rows of four and. then switch round two buttons.

Spoon button ♀

Lay a tablespoon on the ground, ideally on well-trodden sand. Each player now receives three to five buttons of the same colour, and takes it in turn to throw them from a starting line. If a player hits the spoon and you hear it rattle, they score a point. If they manage to get their button to stay in the spoon they score five points for this extraordinary feat of skill. When all the buttons have been thrown, check whose buttons lie nearest the spoon. Notice that they may not be ones belonging to the winner of most points!

Flour button ⇧

Each player is given a flat plate with a thick layer of flour on it. Somewhere in the flour are some buttons. Everyone has to find the buttons using only their mouth. They have one minute in which to do this. The players have to see how many buttons they can fish out of the flour without being blinded by it.

Figure 56.

Sleepy button ⬠♀

Take a pin and clamp it between the joints of your fore and middle fingers. The pin must rest so firmly between the joints that it is hidden when you bend your fingers. Do a few practice runs.

Explain to your audience that you have a very tired button which you wish to introduce to them. Move your hands around so as to convince everyone that nothing is hidden in them. Place the button against your hand and open your hand. You explain that the button has just woken up for a moment but is on the point of going to sleep again. Loosen the pin a bit and the button will appear to lie down to sleep. Talk to the button, saying that 'he' went to sleep too soon. Tell 'him' that he really must wake up again for the audience. Slide one hand under the other, so that the pin stands up and the button appears to ask sleepily what the matter is. You can make him try once or twice to get up properly and then finally flop down and stay down. Ooh-aahh he is tired!

Standing button ⬠♀

So you think that buttons won't stand up? Well, it is a bit unlikely with one on its own, but if two are put together it should work. See who can do it the most quickly? Have a trial run to start with.

Each player chooses their buttons, preferably taking quite a large number. Starting with two buttons leant against each other in the middle, you now make a whole line of standing buttons stretching out equally to the left and right. When one person thinks they have done enough to win they shout *stop*. If the line breaks you score nothing.

Whose button? ⬠

Five players each choose their favourite button. These buttons are then mixed together on the table. The sixth player then enters the room, looks at the buttons and has to try and give the buttons to the correct owners. The procedure can then be repeated with different buttons and a different player guessing.

66

Board games for buttons

Frustration button ⌂

Lay out 49 buttons in seven rows, each row having seven buttons. Each player takes it in turn to remove two, three or four buttons which lie next to each other in a straight line either vertically or horizontally, but not diagonally. The player who removes the last button is the winner.

You can vary this by taking into account the colour and number of holes of the buttons. Then the rule is to take away two, three or four buttons which have either the same number of holes, or are the same colour.

Button nut ⌂

You will need three piles of twenty different buttons for this guessing-game. The piles must be identical.

The two players sit opposite each other. There should be a screen of cardboard, books etc. between them. Behind this screen each player lays out one of the three heaps of buttons in a well-ordered arrangement. The players then take turns to put their hands into a bag which contains the third heap of buttons. Player A has to find out as quickly as possible which button Player B has taken out of the bag, and vice-versa. This is done by questioning, for example as follows:

Player A: *Has your button got four holes?*
Player B: *No.*

Now Player A can put all the buttons with four holes aside, for they know that it is not one of those. Now it is Player B's turn to ask:

Player B: *Is your button round?*
Player A: *Yes.*

Now Player B can assemble all the round buttons.

Players can ask what colour the button is and what it is made of, but the answer can only be *yes* or *no*. To make this game really exciting the initial assortment should be cunningly selected: the more similar the buttons are, the harder it is to guess, and this makes the game even more fun.

Buttoulette ⌂

Button-roulette is played with three dice and a game-board (see Figure 57), and of course a number of buttons for the chips. You can give the buttons different values according to the colour or shape or number of holes.

The players stake their chips, throw the three dice and count up their winnings. This is done as follows. Count up the total numbers shown on the dice. Then:

For 3 or 18: win tenfold.
For 4, 5, 16, or 17: win fivefold.
For 6, 7, 8, 13, 14, or 15: win treble.
For 9, 10, 11 or 12: win double.
For a Pair of numbers: win fivefold.
For Three of the same numbers: win eightfold.
All Even numbers win double.
All Odd numbers win double.
For 4, 5, 6, 7, or 8: double
For 13, 14, 15, 16, or 17: double.

Players may play no more than five buttons at a time. The dice should be thrown singly, to make it more exciting.

Figure 57 >

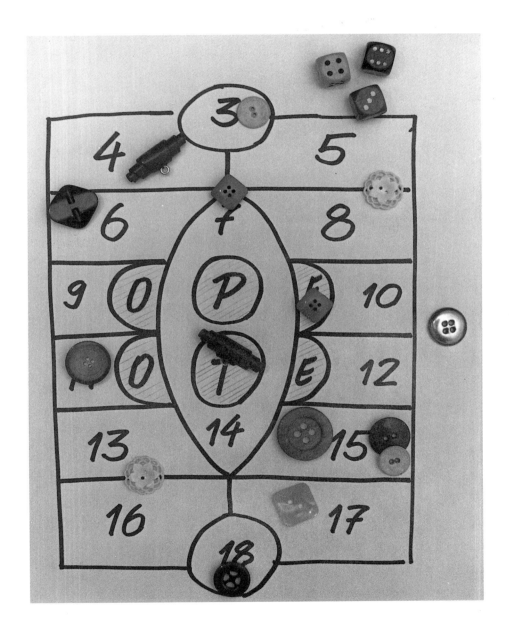

Button ludo ⌂

As you will probably guess, this is a kind of ludo. The squares of the board are cut out of coloured paper and laid together. Dark squares show the starting points, felt-marker circles show the places leading up to the finish. (The squares should be stuck down so that they do not slip.) Surprise, surprise, the game is played with buttons!

Each player chooses the shape and colour of their buttons. The rules are as for ludo, but if a button lands on top of another it does not send that button 'home' but gets carried along with it. The top button can release itself when it wants to, but any buttons trapped underneath cannot. So it is possible to lock in other players' buttons and only release them when you want to. Also you can jump onto your own buttons and move the pile on with one throw of the dice. But each button has to get 'home' by itself.

Star button ⌂

Take four wooden buttons shaped like a boat and arrange them in a cross. Now take four smaller similar buttons and place them between the larger buttons to make a star (see Figure 60). All the buttons should have two holes. The arrangement of buttons takes the place of a board for the game. On the star

Figure 58.

Figure 59.   *Figure 60 >*

there are 24 places: the two holes and the outside point of each button.

Take four pairs of buttons to use as counters. Place each pair at opposite ends of the star. The players take it in turn to throw the dice and to move their counters to score points. The aim of the game is to score as many points as possible. Moves are made as follows:

Throw the dice. Take any button and move it the number of spaces shown on the dice. The moves can be made round the points of the star in a clockwise direction or across the star, along the holes of the boats. In the latter case you can change direction in the middle, but you must continue on a boat of the same size. If a space is already occupied you must pass over it, except when the place is occupied by the twin button. Then you land on the twin and score one point.

If the first player throws a six they cannot move. If they throw a one, two, or three they can move onto the star. If they throw a four they can score a point by moving the button four spaces round the star to land on the twin. If they throw a five they can also score a point by moving their button five spaces straight over the star to land on the twin.

If, apart from your opening throw, you throw a six, instead of moving you may throw again if you wish. If you throw two sixes in succession you can place any button on the centre of the star. This blocks the star so that no-one can cross until another player throws two sixes in succession. They then take the centre button and put it on any place, scoring one point.

The winner is the first player to get six points (or any other number chosen beforehand).

Button chain ⌂

Take five sets of five similar buttons (so a total of 25 buttons). Lay these out in a circle keeping the sets together (each set makes up a fifth of the circle). Each player takes it in turn to throw the dice. They can then move any button to the right or left along the circle, according to the number thrown on the dice. The button will then land on another button which is then removed and put in the first button's original place. The aim is now to move all the buttons around so that a series of five different buttons is created. The player who first succeeds in doing this (by being the player to add the fifth button to a series of four different

Figure 61.   *Figure 62 >*

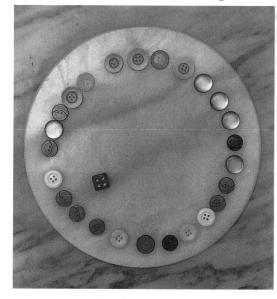

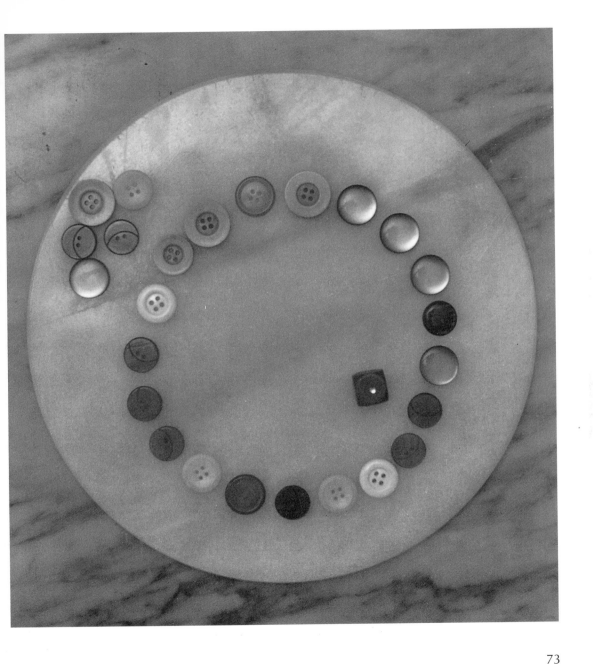

ones) takes this series away and scores five points. Now the gap is closed by making the circle smaller, and the game continues until there are no buttons left.

As you play you will see that the player who wins the second last series also wins the last one, because five different buttons automatically remain.

Button tree ⌂

The button tree board consists of a tree trunk and seven squares round it for the branches (see Figure 63). For this game you need seven sets of four similar buttons, and two dice of different colours. The game is co-operative, so there is no individual winner, but everyone plays against the dice, taking their own risks. It can also be played by one person on their own, as a game of patience.

A special system is used for setting out the buttons at the beginning of the game to ensure the buttons are evenly distributed. Each square is divided into four places and the places are numbered in a series as follows:

Figure 63.

Figure 64.

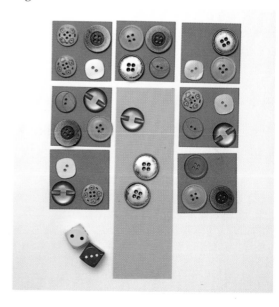

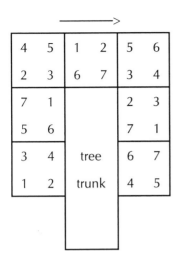

4	5	1	2	5	6
2	3	6	7	3	4
7	1			2	3
5	6			7	1
3	4	tree		6	7
1	2	trunk		4	5

Figure 65.

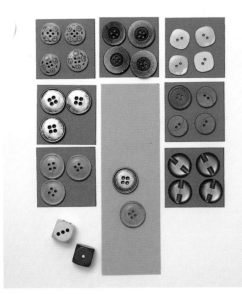

The first four buttons of the first set are placed on the four places numbered 1. The four buttons of the second set are placed on the four places numbered 2 (see Figure 64). Continue in this way until all seven sets have been placed.

The aim of the game is to get each set of four buttons together onto one square. There are two lanes: an outside lane and an inside lane (see Figure 63). The outside lane begins at position 1, bottom left, goes up and round the outside and finishes at position 5, bottom right. The inside lane begins at position 2, bottom left, goes round the inside and finishes at position 4, bottom right. Players move their buttons clockwise along these lanes according to the number they throw on the dice. A button always moves in its own lane and may never cross into another lane.

To free some space for moving, use the tree-trunk as a resting place, in addition to using it as the route to move the buttons from lower right to lower left.

To begin the game throw one of the dice. Count the number of places from the *end* of the lane and move either the inside or the outside button onto the tree trunk.

For example, see Figure 63: you have thrown a four and a one. With the four you can move the white button in the middle right square (position 3 outside lane), or the dark button next to it (position 2 inside lane) onto the tree; and with the three either of the two lower buttons in the same square.

The vacated places are now free for other buttons on a later throw. The buttons on the tree trunk must wait until a place in their lane is free and until the right number has been thrown.

For example, see Figure 64: both the shiny

75

buttons on the trunk belong to the inside lane. If a two is thrown one of them can be placed in the empty space in the first square (position 4). The others have to wait for a free space.

Figure 65 shows a possible situation almost at the end of the game. The silver button on the tree requires a three on the dice to land in the empty space beside the other three silver buttons. The brown button requires a throw of one to land beside the other three brown buttons.

Dance button ⌂

Each player receives the same selection of six different buttons which they lay in front of them, in a single file stretching towards the centre of the table. It does not matter which button is closest to each player, or which button is nearer the centre. Additionally put another series of the same selection of six different buttons in a circle in the middle of the table. Place a cube-shaped button as a dancing button on one of these buttons.

Figure 66.

The first player throws the dice. If they throw a six, they can take away their first button (the one furthest from them). If they throw any other number they move the cube button clockwise round the button circle according to the number shown on the dice. If the cube lands on a type of button which a player has closest to the centre, the player can remove the button. It is now the next player's turn. The winner is the one who is the first to remove all their buttons.

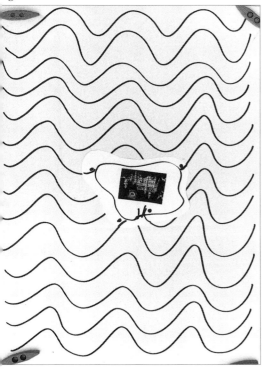

Figure 67.

Ships and treasure ⌂

Some time or another everyone catches 'button-game-fever.' Buttons stimulate one to invent one's own games. Here's an example.

Paint some waves on a piece of card (see Figure 67). Paint an island, perhaps with a palace on it, in the middle. On this island lie glittering treasures, in the form of buttons, waiting for ships to come and get them.

Each player owns a ship. Each ship starts at its own corner of the board (the pirate's cove). The players take turns to throw the dice and move their ships along the crests of the waves, forwards, backwards or sideways, but not diagonally, according to the number thrown on the dice (each crest counts as one space). The object of the game is to sail to the island, load on one single treasure (a button), and sail back to the safety of your pirate's cove. Ships may block each other, but they may not jump over each other (whoever heard of ships flying through the air?). Further rules can be made up yourselves.

U-Button ⌂

This is a game with dice for three players.

Each player chooses three buttons. A board is drawn on a piece of cardboard as in Figure 68. You can vary the size of the U (and consequently the length of the game) but you must always have three squares beside each other.

The players place their buttons in three rows beside each other at the beginning of the course (see Figure 68). The player with the outside row begins by throwing the dice and moving their buttons according to the number thrown. This number can be split among the buttons (for instance if a player throws a six they could move each of their buttons two places). The button can be moved one place forward or diagonally, or it can jump over one other button to an empty square. (For example, the first move could be as follows: the middle button of the outside row jumps over the front button, or it could jump diagonally over the front button of the centre row to land in front of the front button of the inside row.)

After the first player has thrown and moved, it is the centre player's turn, and then the inside player's turn. The aim is to bring all three buttons into a row at the end of the U (see Figure 70).

Figure 68.

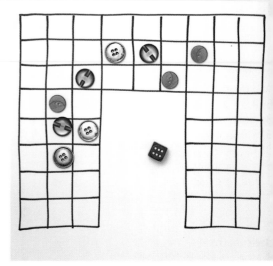

∧ Figure 69.

∨ Figure 70.

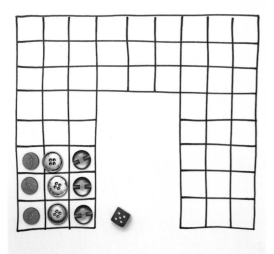

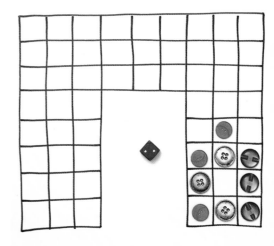

78

Index

⌂ Indoors ♀ Outdoors ✤ Get-to-know ① Games for one ↔ Games for two ✳ Games for many ❒ Board games

⌂ Indoors   ♀ Outdoors   ❖ Get-to-know   ① Games for one   ↔ Games for two   ✳ Games for many   ❐ Board games